My Pinup

Hilton Als

My Pinup

a paean to Prince

A NEW DIRECTIONS
PAPERBOOK ORIGINAL

First published as New Directions Paperbook 1545 in 2022
Manufactured in the United States of America

Library of Congress Cataloging-in-Publication Data
Names: Als, Hilton, author.
Title: My pinup : a paean to Prince / Hilton Als.
Description: [First edition.] | New York : New Directions Publishing, 2022.
Identifiers: LCCN 2022028205 | ISBN 9780811234498 (paperback) |
ISBN 9780811234504 (ebook)
Subjects: LCSH: Prince—Criticism and interpretation. | Als, Hilton. |
Sex role in music.
Classification: LCC ML420.P974 A75 2022 |
DDC 781.66092—dc23/eng/20220722
LC record available at https://lccn.loc.gov/2022028205

10 9 8 7 6 5 4 3 2 1

New Directions Books are published for James Laughlin
by New Directions Publishing Corporation
80 Eighth Avenue, New York 10011

If I Was Your Girlfriend

Dick jokes, ass jokes, black-women-versus-white-women jokes, Taliban jokes, Whitney Houston jokes, more sex jokes, and then, finally, the best joke of all, because it plays like a confession telegraphed directly out of the comedian's subconscious. From Jamie Foxx's 2002 television stand-up special, *I Might Need Security*: "Hollywood is freaky . . . You get the chance to meet all your, you know, your favorite stars when you're in Hollywood. And I met Prince . . . the man, you know what I'm sayin'?" Applause.

Jamie Foxx, dressed in a blue shirt with a satin sheen and dark trousers, his considerable ass in the air, traverses the stage, a pin spot following him as he follows his thoughts. "I'm not no fag," he continues, almost bashfully. "But uh. I mean, he's cute, he pretty . . . I just ain't never seen no man that look like that. Just dainty and shit." Beat. Hangdog expression. "I couldn't look at him in his eyes." Because "this little pretty bitch . . . came out with a little ice-skating outfit on, you know? With the boots sewn into the shit. And I'm like, That's nice . . . I'm not gay. I'm just saying *that's nice*." More existential shrugging of the shoulders, turning away from the audience, embarrassment and confusion as Foxx's desire attaches itself to a different, or rather unexpected, form. This is America, after all, where for sex to be sex it needs to be shaming. He flashes his goofy overbite. "I know you thinking—you thinking I'm gay," Foxx says, more to his own heart and mind, perhaps, than to anyone in the audience. "I'm just saying I challenge any dude in here not to look in his eyes and feel some kind of shit . . . 'Cause he was pretty. He looked like a deer or something, or a fawn . . . I shouldn't even be telling you this shit." More laughter from the audience, more abashment from Foxx.

Then Foxx recalls how Prince started "talking with that shit"—adding a little audio to his distinctive visuals. Prince's speaking voice—which Foxx's audience may or may not know from a thousand and one uncandid interviews on VH1 and the like, or an awards show, or something—belies his slight frame: it's deep and steady with few inflections. In any case, Foxx is spot-on when he imitates it. Foxx as Prince, utterly cool: "So how's everything going?" Foxx as himself, his eyes downcast: "You know . . ." As Prince: "I heard you and LL [Cool J, the rapper who costarred with Foxx in Oliver Stone's *Any Given Sunday* (1999)] got into it . . . What do you think Jesus would have done in that situation?" Foxx, again as himself: "I don't know. Knuckle up." Laughter. And then, shaking off his Prince impersonation: "I glanced in his eyes once." After a while, defiantly: "Okay, yeah. Okay, I was a fag for two seconds. But I wasn't on the bottom of the shit, I was on top, don't get it twisted . . . I'd have fucked the shit out of that motherfucker. That troubled me though, man . . . When I left, the security guard knew something was wrong with me. He was like, 'What's up playa? . . . You looked in his eyes, didn't you?'" Foxx admits, sheepishly, that he did. He is so confused. Freeing his mind—will his ass follow? And then what? Will he be a fag, forever desperate to stare up into Prince's up, who called Prince "Miss." Why did he want to leave us for that nonworld of convention he seemed to aspire to, where "she" got married to a woman who looked like her, then, to make matters worse, dressed as Miles Davis had while on tour promoting his rock-jazz fusion album *Bitches Brew*? Why did he want to betray the colored queer in himself?

At parties in New York, uptown and down, I stopped dancing when frat boys pumped their fists in the air to "1999," or slid across the floor when "Kiss" came on, or grabbed their obliging girl-friends—girls unlike the fierce dykes who sang and played backup for Prince in his early years—and twirled them around to "Raspberry Beret." They didn't know what he meant by any of it, but his queers did, and yet I no longer mattered; what mattered was Prince's acquisition of a larger audience, those people who purchased records and filled concert halls, not the black queens who lip-synched to "Sister" while voguing near the Hudson River in the clear light of night. But in 1988, Prince re-deemed himself—somewhat. That year, he released *Lovesexy*; the record made things different again. It was as if Lazarus had risen from some strange frat-boy-populated cave. The cover told us everything:

it was Prince, naked, his hair feathered, one hand shielding a beautiful nipple. The album featured another female doppelgänger—Cat, a dancer and singer who looked like Prince insofar as anyone could look like Prince. She was spectacular in ways that Prince felt he had to own during his *Purple Rain* reign. You could see it in the music videos. He performed, but Cat *worked*. But he was still too much the showman and the Boss Man not to upstage her.

Cat was beautiful. She had a big ass. She posed on the Thunderbird that Prince and his cohort partied on at the end of the show. With her long, curly hair and well-toned biceps, Cat was the girl Prince had been before he stopped being a girl: outrageous and demanding. She rapped to the audience. She got right in our collective face; you could see her eyeliner. Prince smiled behind his guitar, behind his own shimmering ass as Cat became him and sang his lyrics: a twinning for the ages. Cat was not only Prince, she was Cynthia and Rosie from Sly's Family Stone, Betty Davis without Miles. I longed for that twinning. I longed to be the Prince to someone's Cat, and the other way around, too. Like a figure in a Platonic dialogue, I had always longed to meet my other half, my Prince half, and then another, and

S ir?" the young black security guard said tentatively. There was a pause, followed by a barely audible response from the room beyond. All around, one could hear the grumblings of trunks being wheeled this way and that and of the gaffers and food-service people and sound engineers setting up for another show. The venue: St. Louis's Savvis Center. The artist: Prince Rogers Nelson. The occasion: the 2004 tour for his album *Musicology*, his first to reach *Billboard*'s top five since ♀, in 1992.

St. Louis was the twenty-sixth stop on the American tour for *Musicology*, which a number of industry insiders were calling Prince's comeback after years of hassles with his former record company,

Warner Bros., and of artistic floundering as well. He was reemerging from under all that as an artist of present-day significance and clout, without which significance and clout he could become—as less gifted and less tenacious musicians of his generation already had—(at best) a legend who worked occasionally or (at worst) a creepy novelty act.

Outside, the May air was thick. Inside, the air was thick, too, but with anticipation—over what Prince might demand or suddenly require from the seclusion of his dressing room. His dressing room was located a floor below the auditorium proper, where, in just under two and a half hours, many, many people would converge with the happy expectation of demanding *something* from him.

When I saw Prince at Madison Square Garden on the *Lovesexy* tour, in 1988, he wore a halter top and tight little pants. He danced, and his behind danced with him. In the colored world, a big ass is part of one's physiology, one's legacy. I could only show my ass with my mouth—that is, through language. Which felt distinctly different from Prince's mouth and ass that fucked us up so beautifully in performance. Prince was showing his booty again, and everyone in the audience could taste it once again. Once done, he had the black-queen vote in his pocket again: he was dressed in the height of tranny wear.

But that didn't last long. He wanted to be a boy

and play in the world of corporate politics. He split with his record label, albums were released under other names, all that twisted righteousness forsaken so Prince could approximate being less a freak and more a man in the eyes of those men he disparaged but must have admired for what they had: power. Maybe Prince was trying on power like he'd try on garters or fishnets. But he didn't jettison the suits—or his suit—fast enough to win me back. And if it hadn't been for the love of others, I might never have forgiven him. So until I met him, I saw Prince only through other people—when I saw him at all. He was like a bride who had left me at the altar of difference to embrace the expected. Could my queer heart ever let any of this go, and forgive him?

I saw the *Lovesexy* show with a boy I was very much taken with who was not as taken with me. I made him a peach pie I thought we might like to eat during the performance, but the performance irked him: it took away from the drama of his *I, I, I*. He loved Prince but not his power. And that is what it must always have been like for Prince: Black queen (if only in spirit), how dare you walk into the room and suck us all up in you? How dare you suggest, as you did in "Controversy," that you were neither male nor female but possess the power of both? Can't you see I'm here? A white queer (or straight) man sitting here, the natural custodian of the world's attention? What gives you, Prince, the right to take that spotlight away from me and shine it on that fine ass of yours, which no flat-assed white man could ever hope to approximate, let alone compete with? The pie grew sticky in my lap. He refused to eat it.

No love is perfect. But in that relationship there was so little to hold on to I focused on what I could, like pie crust. The pie crust at Prince's concert was white and nasty. During the time Prince was on his *Lovesexy* tour, and Cat was being some version of it-self, New York was wrapped in its own self-congrat-ulatory arms, and tatted on it was political correct-ness. Prince showed his ass, and liberals thought every other black person should, too, given their history of oppression—but at a distance, maybe from a stage: they didn't want all that funk in their faces. I resented this well-meaning, condescend-ing attitude even as I benefited from it by having a sensitive, "understanding" white boyfriend. But he wasn't my boyfriend. A little flirting, one night of heavy petting, but talking about the projects we were meant to do, the stories I would write for him for the films he wanted to make. But nothing much came of this talk. We were always watching to see who could give less. That was our erotics. I had language I could withhold, while he had a body he could withhold. The odd thing was, I couldn't stop working for his hoped-for love, just as he couldn't stop hanging around me for some kind of approval, for validation. Eventually, it all fell apart. One day, after knowing one another for a year or two, I made a date with him to say goodbye—I was going to Berlin with a friend—and he showed up with a man he had been seeing. I paid him back for disrupting the rhythm of our mutual pain by denying him the thing he loved most about me: my language. And my ability to listen to all his dreams—and that's what Prince wanted me to do, too!

cry, He is coming / Don't die without knowing the cross"), he had also written of the threat of Armaggeddon as being a second chance at life ("War is all around us / My mind says prepare 2 fight / So if I gotta die / I'm gonna listen 2 my body tonight").

This was not new. Prince's best songs, like those of a number of artists of color before him (Aretha Franklin, James Brown, Stevie Wonder), have always been an admixture of the sacred (gospel) and the profane (sex). But what Prince has rewritten in his thirty-five-year career—more than thirty solo albums, five movie soundtracks, three starring roles in as many films, appearances in dozens of music videos (some of which he directed himself), as well as production duties on a number of albums by other artists (Sheila E., Sheena Easton, Mavis Staples, Vanity, the Mary Jane Girls, the Time) and the building of Paisley Park, a recording studio in his hometown of Minneapolis, where he lived until recently—are the often racist and homophobic attitudes by which soul music was produced and marketed, not least by black artists themselves.

Unlike Franklin or Brown, however, Prince did not grow up in a predominantly black context, which is to say the Baptist church or its environs.

Sandwiched between Wisconsin and the Dakotas, Minnesota is Laura Ingalls Wilder and Robert Bly territory, home to German and Scandinavian immigrants with a strong Lutheran bent and no black music scene to speak of. Until Prince.

In general, artists forge one of two career paths for themselves early on. Either they reject the world in order to become the romantic hero of their own imagining, or they embrace the real, transmuting what they find in the streets and in people's homes into tales an audience can readily identify with. Growing up, Prince did both. And he used urban black music and black gay attitude as it filtered through and got mixed up in his predominantly white Midwestern environment to express his quintessentially American self. And it was this self—which, visually, at least, he played as male and female, gay and straight, black and white—that Prince used to remake black music in his own image.

Before Prince, black popular music had been limited by its blackness, which is to say its fundamentally Christian, blues-inflected, conservative attitude toward everything pushed in Prince's early shows with his backing band, the Revolution, and in his records: girl-on-girl action, genuine female empowerment based not on suffering but on a love of the body, a racially and thus sonically mixed world. In the 1980s, he sometimes wrote and sang songs by and about "Camille," one of his fictional alter egos. Given Prince's DJ-like mixing of homosexualist and heterosexualist impulses in his early work, it is not overreaching to imagine that Prince thought of race as a similarly fluid component of life. Certainly he never positioned race as a problem, as Sly Stone—certainly the most counterculturally influenced black pop lyricist before Prince—did in his song "Don't Call Me Nigger, Whitey." Stone was writing in a different time, but the real difference was that Prince's politics—again in his early work—were personal, self-referential. (There are exceptions to this, of course, as there are bound to be with any artist who has such a rich and varied catalogue. But of the hundreds of songs Prince has written and performed, only a handful come to mind as overtly political—for example, 1981's "Ronnie, Talk to Russia," about Reagan and Star Wars, and 1987's "Sign 'O' the Times," which deals with drug addiction and poverty, among other themes.)

And when Prince did sing about his personal

surprising synthesis of black soul beats and white rock riffs; if *Musicology* was about anything at all, it was about the nostalgia Prince—and his audience—had for those presampling days when soul was soul, not pasteurized rap, and when Prince had been a phenomenon. And it was either because his audience was older, or Prince was older, or the music industry itself had grown older—and more embattled and more segregated along the way—that Prince, once the most forward-looking of artists, had entered the Negro music ghetto he once disavowed. Now he even dressed the part. Maybe he stopped showing his ass because of God. For, in addition to the more conventional aspects of black music and style he now embraced, Prince had also taken the Lord as his personal savior. He was a Jehovah's Witness. Maybe he wouldn't be left behind after all.

"You want some water or something?" Prince asked. He was standing in front of a table stocked with bottles of juice, soda, and water. And I almost laughed out loud, remembering what Prince had done with water in his old songs: as a set piece between Wendy and Lisa in 1984's *Purple Rain* ("Wendy?" "Yes, Lisa." "Is the water warm enough?" "Yes, Lisa." "Shall we begin?") and as a womanist-identified element on the vastly under-rated album *Lovesexy* (1988). It took me a moment to retrieve the bottle of water, which he extended to me without turning around. I saw his face on a computer monitor flickering in the room before I saw his actual face. The screen faded in and out of promotional material pertaining to *Musicology*. The security guard recused himself. He did not imme-diately close the door behind him, which was just as well: the dressing room was relatively small and dark, and the light from the hall fell on the com-puter monitor and a keyboard resting near it, and on the table laden with beverages, and also on an-other table stocked with fruit and cheese and crack-ers placed kitty-corner to the first.

Both tables had been draped in black and pur-ple fabrics. There was a leather couch against the wall facing the two tables; on either side of it was a roomy leather chair. Candles flickered on various surfaces. And as if to complement the room—or have the room complement him—Prince was in black and purple, too. He was shoeless, dressed in dark tropical wool trousers and a black vest with wide lapels. The vest was cinched tightly around his waist. Under the vest he wore a purple shirt.

Purple has played a significant role in Prince's lexicon as a songwriter and haberdasher—his song (and album, and debut film) "Purple Rain," for instance, as well as a slew of lyrics throughout the years ("All of my purple life, I've been looking for a dame / That would wanna be my wife / That was my intention, babe / If we cannot make babies, maybe we can make some time"), to say nothing of his penchant for sporting purple footwear, guitars, and suits (the comedian Sandra Bernhard has referred to him, with reverence, as "The Purple Paisley God"). But as with so much about Prince, there has been no explanation for his fixation. However, the color is associated with royalty, spirituality, mystery—and mourning.

The darkness in the dressing room acted as a kind of veil that obscured his veil of shyness. I sat down in a corner of the sofa. Prince didn't deign to join me at first. With his back to me still, he drifted over to the food table, as if in search of something he wasn't sure he had asked for. And not finding it there, had no choice but to sit down. He positioned himself on one of the leather chairs to the left of the sofa, his posture a caricature of weariness. I was immediately transfixed by his slight frame; his straightened hair, cut relatively short, but curled, added an additional one or two inches. (Prince stands 5'4" tall.) There was more silence, and as it unfolded, I took in his face, which had the exact shape, and large eyes, of a beautiful turtle. I asked him about his film career, which had received relatively short shrift next to his music. Suddenly animated, he said: "With film, you have to sit around a table with a bunch of other folk, talking about *when* you're doing the project, as opposed to doing the project. There are so many factors that don't have anything to do with what you want to do—and they never stick to the original vision. If a movie could be made in a shorter period of time, who knows? But there are too many people involved in all that. So," he trailed off, half smiling at the memory, perhaps, of meetings and shoots and the rest. "What I prefer to do now is focus on the kind of stuff you can do—music and videos and records—with the New Power Generation." He was referring not only to the name of his band (which had changed lineup countless times since its creation in the late 1970s) but to the entire constellation of Prince-generated products that went by the name, along with a website on which he sold albums from his back catalogue, a live boxed set that he had produced himself, and so on.

Since the termination of his contract with Warner Bros. in 1996, Prince set about—with the same Mephistophelian (or Faustian, depending on who you talked to) energy he had always been known for—building an industry unto himself, the better to protect his music and his image. "Once, I was standing around with Stevie Wonder—this was early on—and I was like, 'Stevie, do you own all your own masters? Does Sly?'" Recalling Wonder's response, Prince looked slightly pained. "And Stevie said he didn't. And none of the musicians I had grown up with—the guys who taught *me*—had any money, because they didn't own what they created. So how can you trust anyone in this business when they don't respect you even when it comes to . . . business?" He chuckled almost noiselessly, then went on: "*Remember, your friends are never on your payroll.* When I wrote the word slave on my face, it wasn't because I felt I was a slave to the record company but because I had to earn back what I'd *already* earned—which was the music."

According to Michele Anthony, former president of Sony Music, *Musicology*'s distributor, Prince interviewed a number of record-company executives for the album, which was more or less finished and packaged by the time he came knocking. She told me that artists are not usually given a distribution deal without the record company having a say in all aspects of production—music videos, publicity, advertising—and retaining ownership of the masters. "Because when you own the masters, the music has a life past the CD. For instance, if people want to sample the music or use it in a commercial or whatever, they have to go through you and pay you for fair use—profits that you share with the artist."

Despite the blurring in today's music industry of the boundaries surrounding a piece of music's ownership—let alone its authorship—record companies still assist with the manufacturing and shipping of records to as many retailers as still exist. Even though Prince's Paisley Park studio produced a number of records by a number of artists—Chaka Khan, Larry Graham, and Mavis Staples among them—in those predigital days he simply didn't have the resources to advertise and distribute these records as widely as they should have been. They unprecedented. The albums counted on charts overwhelmingly were sold in *stores*—but albums sold were albums sold, no matter the venue or the price (*Billboard* soon changed its rules to foil Prince's tactic). In short, Prince was selling the album the best way he knew how: by selling himself—his new, heterosexualized, Jesus-loving self. As befit the times.

"It's not as if they're willing to give it up to *us* because we're *us*," Prince said to me, rather conspiratorially. I took "us" to mean black people. "We've always had to work that way. The question is: Where's our forty acres and a mule?" We both laughed. I thought about a moment in James Baldwin's essay about Richard Wright:

> He had a trick, when he greeted me, of saying "Hey, boy!" with a kind of pleased, surprised expression on his face. It was very friendly and it was also, faintly, mockingly conspiratorial— as though we were two black boys, in league against the world, and had just managed to spirit away several loads of watermelon.

Prince then said, even more conspiratorially, "Lauryn [Hill] called me." Hill, as almost everyone knew by then, had stalled after her 1998 Grammy-winning solo album, *The Miseducation of Lauryn Hill*. (She had released a live follow-up album in 2002 that was scorned by critics.) Bad press and a number of lawsuits from collaborators who felt they had not been properly remunerated or credited for their work plagued her. The latter problem was one Prince had dealt with on a number of occasions. "And I told her she wouldn't have to deal with all of that if she came and recorded with us. She could record with us. *And* keep her masters."

"I don't think Joni Mitchell"—whose complex lyrics and chord progressions Prince has acknowledged as having influenced his—"owns her masters, either," I said. "Imagine if she did."

Prince said: "She'd be Oprah."

Just then, two members of Prince's current band—Renato Neto, a Hispanic keyboardist, and the legendary black horn player and James Brown alumnus Maceo Parker—entered the room. Prince smiled sweetly when he saw Maceo—a smile I saw him confer most often when older black men sought him out.

Maceo, courtly, said that he and Renato wanted to play an arrangement that they had worked on. Prince sat quietly, rapt. After the two men finished playing, there was a moment of silence. Then Prince said, "I liked it better the other way. When you played it the other way, I cried." After they departed, Prince turned to me, his large eyes suddenly growing larger, and he said: "I'm having an epiphany! What if you called your office and say you're not writing the article, that you're writing a book with me instead?" In his enthusiasm, Prince bounded out of the chair he had been sitting in, seized by the hope he found in another potential collaboration. When I expressed some ambivalence, Prince smiled, undeterred, suddenly as demure as in Jamie Foxx's subconscious. I could not look at Prince. Nor could I look away. He said: "Why don't you come back after the show? There's some people I'd like you to meet." After I agreed, I asked Prince what his relationship was to the press in general, perhaps as a way of asking what his interest in me was in particular. And he said, growing contemplative, "The males are not so nice to me. Not as nice as the females." And after I asked him why he thought this was so, he said: "Afraid of their feminine side, I guess."

as much ease as he offered me a bottle of water. He teased the packed house with: "And who said I couldn't fill a stadium?" The audience roared as he played one song after another, a brilliant medley of wit and musicianship taking us higher. I tried not to love him more than I already did; after all, I was a reporter. But as much as the reporter was there, so too there was myself—and another and another self—and none of us could help but be amazed that this was happening after the show: going backstage, and then leaving because I didn't know who to contact, but then a girl was running after us, saying, "Mister! Mister! Prince wants to see you!" She was plump, lovely, and dark, and out of breath, saying, "He would have *killed* me if I didn't find you!" Then she escorted me to a room where Prince was getting his makeup refreshed moments after the show, and he said, turning his beautiful turtle head to me when he saw me, "Hey," and then, to his makeup artist: "Put on number 14." Meaning the eyelashes he wanted to put on for a little post-show conference. He was my Dorothy Parker. After that, I waited outside Prince's room while he went in to set something up. When I was asked in, I found Prince sitting on the sofa with funk legend Larry Graham, and Graham's wife. They were all holding Bibles. They wanted to talk to me about Jehovah, and what it meant to be a Jehovah's Witness.

We weren't in that semidark room long, or more specifically, I can't remember all that we said; I tend to go blank when it comes to Jesus. What I remember is the specificity of their feeling. Their certainty that Jehovah was the way, and what I remember, too, is how pretty and little Prince looked in relation to the Grahams. Because they weren't friends so much as parents, and was he maybe looking for a true brother? Had he been looking for one, and another and another, his whole life? Presently a guard told him it was time to go to the after party. Apparently they had bought out a bar downtown. By the time I arrived, Prince was already there, and he had someone bring me over. It was like being on a date, in that there were parents to negotiate between us. Prince's parents were tall black men, but after he called me over to a booth where he sat with other men, he didn't stay seated for long. He walked over to the bar with me, but he wasn't drinking: he was looking at footage of the concert he'd just performed. It played on a monitor over the bar. He started dancing along to himself dancing on the video. I asked him if he'd eaten anything—like a parent, or a brother, calling their child or little brother to the table. If you stood close enough to him, that's what you wanted to do—nourish him, become the family he'd left so long ago. He told me he'd eat something later, on the bus, and the next thing I knew he was on the bus, and I was going to see the next show in Nashville, but not before his publicist called me and asked me if I wanted to live in Paisley Park and write a book with him, given his feelings.

I knew that if I went to Minneapolis I would never come back. How many pies would I make for him, hoping to fatten him up. But I did all of that anyway, and not in Minneapolis. After Nashville, Prince, I retuned to New York, and to the man whose girlfriend I wanted to be. I wanted to be his Dorothy Parker, and his O Sister. You know what I mean, Prince. I wanted to make him scrambled eggs, and I did. I could not make a poem out of any of it. Dorothy Parker, dark-haired, helmet-haired, was never a waitress like in your song, Prince, but she wrote some poems—not like yours. You can't write everything. In any case, you got certain things about her right in your do-rag'd head, and then you put them in your song, lines like "(Dorothy Parker was cool)" and "Well, earlier I'd been talkin' stuff / In a violent room / Fighting with lovers past / I needed someone with a quicker wit than mine / Dorothy was fast." Those people in the violent room were phantoms, I know, Prince, the ghosts of fingers past on your back, your neck, pushing your head toward the paper, forcing you to remember their old love—it keeps them alive, as my old loves keep me alive by forcing my hand, which writes lines like these.

In 1994, six years after I met him and knew at once I wanted to live with him, and five years after I realized I wanted to be his Dorothy Parker, we went to see Jennifer Jason Leigh in *Mrs. Parker and the Vicious Circle*. I was jealous of Jennifer Jason Leigh's fringe, largely because he loved it; he also loved the fact that Parker left her estate to the NAACP. Negroes like you, Prince, benefited from her funny business. I was not his Dorothy Parker. I did not have the language or enough distance from language to be sentimental or amusing or cruel in conversation, as Dorothy Parker was known to have been. Sometimes men enjoy that—a girl who turns on love like a dime. It means that girl has the control, can take them by the balls, mother them, or leave them brain-fried and dry. I could not be his girl. I did not have control. I did not write verse. I did not think there was any need: there was him. Wasn't that poem enough? I walked by his side. This was years ago. I did not speak. I told him everything, but not really. I saw his skin color. It was like yours, Prince. I saw his thinness. It was like yours, Prince. I saw his difference. It was like yours, Prince. Was I in love with him or with you when I met you backstage in St. Louis or saw you in Texas? Was he in you? He laughed so hard when those boys climbed on top of you in the video for "Gett Off." Did I look as laughable to him as I tried—clumsily—to climb on top of him? He looked so lonely! As lonely as you could and did look to me, Prince; I knew your false eyelashes weren't any company at all.

I met him when *Lovesexy* came out. We worked at the same advertising agency. I was drawn to him because he was irrefutably colored in a "professional" world where no one wanted to understand that, let alone translate it. The rings and head rags, understanding George Herriman, more than getting Zora Neale Hurston's style. I have always loved translating. When I was little my younger brother did not speak. I told the world—our mother—what he wanted, what he might be thinking, based on the permutations of his silence. Later, as a student, I translated what authors meant in their novels. What a lady's train meant in one chapter, what her tears meant in another. But to return to our story: Within weeks my Princelike friend and I were out in the clubs. Those clubs looked the way New York felt then: poor and dirty and permanently crepuscular as we all danced under pain of death (AIDS) or smoked cigarettes dipped in brown junk. In those clubs the lights went down or were turned up bright; a siren blared and hands shot up. I inched closer to him as he danced to you, Prince. But already he was you, Prince, in my mind. He had the same coloring, and the same loneliness I wanted to fill with my admiration. I couldn't love him enough. We were colored boys together. There is not enough of that in the world, Prince—but you know that. Still, when other people see that kind of fraternity they want to kill it. But we were so committed to each other, we never could work out what that violence meant. There was so much love between us. Why didn't anyone want us to share it? We wanted to have a good time. Our good time: reading Adrienne Kennedy and Gertrude Stein, looking at pictures but I moved away right quick: I was a sad bug crawling in the folds of his Princelike harem pants, or the wrong light combed through his "good" Princelike hair. In 2005 he moved away from me to spare me my love—perhaps. But it was too late. I was married to him, forever. In between meeting him and his leaving, I met you, Prince, but you were already gone as you talked to me because he was gone.

Where did you two go off to, Prince? In those years—the years he was my brother and I wanted him to ask if I might be his girlfriend—I introduced him to a woman who eventually became his Dorothy Parker, a woman who, in fact, had sometimes worked as a waitress and sometimes sported a fringe and didn't have enough distance from language to be a wit but was an observer. I introduced him to her because I knew he needed a woman, Prince, in the way maybe you need a woman, a Dorothy Parker. My female friend held fast to his love, Prince, and she held fast to me. She made him scrambled eggs, and he ate those too. He liked them better than my limp and rubbery eggs, but who knows. He ate all the eggs that were put before him. He took photographs of her because he did not want to misremember her in his love;